New Year's Day

by Mari C. Schuh

Consulting Editor: Gail Saunders-Smith, Ph.D.

Consultant: Alexa Sandmann, Ed.D.
Professor of Literacy
The University of Toledo
Member, National Council for the Social Studies

Pebble Books

an imprint of Capstone Press
Mankato, Minnesota

Pebble Books are published by Capstone Press
151 Good Counsel Drive, P.O. Box 669, Mankato, Minnesota 56002
http://www.capstone-press.com

1 2 3 4 5 6 07 06 05 04 03 02

Library of Congress Cataloging-in-Publication Data
Schuh, Mari C., 1975–
    New Year's Day / by Mari C. Schuh.
    p. cm.—(Holidays and celebrations)
    Summary: Simple text and photographs describe the history of New Year's
Day and the many ways in which it is celebrated.
    Includes bibliographical references and index.
    ISBN 0-7368-1446-9 (hardcover)
    ISBN 0-7368-9400-4 (paperback)
    1. New Year—Juvenile literature. [1. New Year. 2. Holidays.] I. Title. II. Series.
GT4905 .S35   2003
394.2614—dc21
                                                                    2002000089

Note to Parents and Teachers

The Holidays and Celebrations series supports national social
studies standards related to culture. This book describes New Year's
Day and illustrates how it is celebrated in North America. The
photographs support early readers in understanding the text. The
repetition of words and phrases helps early readers learn new
words. This book also introduces early readers to subject-specific
vocabulary words, which are defined in the Words to Know section.
Early readers may need assistance to read some words and to use
the Table of Contents, Words to Know, Read More, Internet Sites,
and Index/Word List sections of the book.

Table of Contents

January						
S	M	T	W	T	F	S
			1	2	3	4
5	6	7	8	9	10	11
12	13	14	15	16	17	18
19	20	21	22	23	24	25
26	27	28	29	30	31	

4

New Year's Day is on January 1. It is the first day of the new year.

New Year's Day is one
of the oldest holidays.
It was first celebrated
by people who lived
thousands of years ago.
They celebrated a
new planting season.

Today people start celebrating on the night before New Year's Day. The night before is called New Year's Eve. New Year's Eve is always on December 31.

Some people have parties on New Year's Eve. They eat food and listen to music. Some people wear costumes or masks.

Other people watch television on New Year's Eve. They watch the party and fireworks at Times Square in New York City.

Most people try to
stay awake until midnight.
That is when the old
year is done and the
new year begins.

People celebrate at midnight.
They throw confetti and
blow party horns.

Most people do not have to work or go to school on New Year's Day. Some people watch football games. Others watch parades.

Many people make New Year's resolutions. They write down their goals for the new year. They hope to make the new year better.

Words to Know

confetti—small pieces of colored paper; people throw confetti at parties, parades, and other celebrations.

costume—clothes people wear to hide who they are; people wear costumes for fun at parties.

fireworks—rockets that make loud noises and display colorful lights when they explode in the sky

resolution—a promise to yourself that you will try hard to do something; people often make resolutions for New Year's Day.

Times Square—a small part of New York City; the world's largest New Year's Eve party is in Times Square.

Read More

Erlbach, Arlene. *Happy New Year, Everywhere!* Brookfield, Conn.: Millbrook Press, 2000.

Marx, David F. *New Year's Day.* Rookie Read-About Holidays. New York: Children's Press, 2000.

Rau, Dana Meachen. *New Year's Day.* A True Book. New York: Children's Press, 2000.

Internet Sites

BrainPOP: New Year's
http://www.brainpop.com/specials/
newyears/index.weml

Happy New Year!
http://wilstar.com/holidays/newyear.htm

Happy New Year Coloring Pages
http://www.coloring.ws/newyears.htm

Index/Word List

Word Count: 190
Early-Intervention Level: 14

Credits
Heather Kindseth, series designer; Patrick D. Dentinger, book designer,
    Wanda Winch, photo researcher; Nancy White, photo stylist

Capstone Press/Gary Sundermeyer, cover, 1, 4, 8, 14, 16
Corbis/Leng/Leng, 10
Countdown Entertainment, 12 (inset)
International Stock/Patrick Ramsey, 20
North Wind Picture Archives, 6
Tournament of Roses/Long Photography, 18
Unicorn Stock Photos/Tom McCarthy, 12